THE KU-KLUX KLAN

Rev. James M. Gillis, C.S.P.

THE KU-KLUX KLAN

BY REV. JAMES M. GILLIS, C.S.P.

HE most curious combination of comedy and tragedy, of melodrama and burlesque, of buffoonery and villainy that has appeared in America, is the Ku-Klux Klan. At this late date in the history of the world, it is difficult to achieve distinction in the commission of crime. But the Klan has at least achieved peculiarity. It combines nonsense with murder. If one were to meet a mob of Klansmen leading their victim to a whipping party or a tarring and feathering "bee," one might imagine, from their appearance and their antics, that they were a class of sophomores hazing a freshman. Even as they built a fire and heated their irons, to brand their victim with the insignia, K. K. K., one might imagine that they were still joking. The proceedings might be only an initiation into a college fraternity. When the jokers have frightened the candidate to "within an inch of his life," surely, one might think, they will suddenly laugh at him and let him go. Here and now, so far away from Fiji or Borneo or the Cannibal Islands, and so long after Cotton Mather and the human bonfires at Salem, it seems incredible that men could sear the flesh of a fellow human being, or actually burn him alive. Incredible, but it is true. One of the paradoxes of civilization is that in this land of libraries and schools and churches, in the era of the automobile and the aëroplane and the radio, it is still possible for men to put a human being in a steel cage,

1

and roast him, while they dance around the fire, shouting, laughing, merrymaking as if at a barbecue. It is still more paradoxical—and more humiliating—that America is the only land in which such atrocities really take place. The Bolsheviki do not burn people alive. Canadian soldiers were not crucified by the Germans in Belgium. Even the inferential insult to Tahiti and Borneo must, on second thought, be withdrawn. No such things are done in the Cannibal Islands as are done in Texas and Georgia and Alabama, and in some more northerly States. The Ku-Klux Klan is indeed a malignant phenomenon.

But—again the curious combination—the Klan is none the less ridiculous. Even in the act of crime, the Klansmen act like clowns. The murder-gang masquerades as a Halloween party. Therein lies its chief distinction. Therein, also, is one of the difficulties of dealing with it. We need a champion to fight against the Klansmen. But if we could choose our champion, from the living or the dead, I hesitate to say whether we should summon Daniel Webster or Mark Twain. Webster would thunder at them. Mark Twain would make game of them. And—for the moment at least—I think that the humorist would be more efficient than the statesman and orator. One thing is certain. If we do not laugh at the Klansmen, the rest of the world will laugh at us. As a caricature of America, the Klan is infinitely more absurd than *Main Street*. Babbitt is not nearly so preposterous as William Joseph Simmons,[1] the "Imperial Wizard."

As is always the case with those who appeal to the

[1] William Joseph Simmons later was succeeded by a man named Clarke. Clarke was ousted and Simmons became a second time head of the order. In November 1922, Simmons was "kicked upstairs," being given the title, "Emperor for Life." The present Imperial Wizard is H. W. Evans.

sense of humor in others, without having any humor in themselves, the masters of the Klan are never so funny as when they are most solemn. Their ritual is claptrap. Their sacred ceremonies are extravaganza. Their official documents are "highfalutin," "bunkum." Witness this grandiloquent salutatory of the "Imperial Wizard" to his worshipful underlings:

The Most Sublime Lineage in all History,
Commemorating and Perpetuating the Most Dauntless Organization Known to Man.

IMPERIAL PALACE
KNIGHTS OF THE KU-KLUX KLAN
INCORPORATED
ATLANTA, GEORGIA

To all Genii, Grand Dragons, and Hydras of Realms, Grand Goblins and Kleagles of Domains, Grand Titans and Furies of Provinces, Giants, Exalted Cyclops and Terrors of Klantons, and to all citizens of the Invisible Empire, Knights of the Ku-Klux Klan—in the name of our valiant, venerated Dead, I affectionately greet you. . . .

And the conclusion of the same manifesto:

Done in the Aulic of his Majesty, Imperial Wizard, Emperor of the Invisible Empire, Knights of the Ku-Klux Klan, in the Imperial City of Atlanta, on this the ninth day of the ninth month of the year of Our Lord, 1921, and on the Dreadful Day of the Weeping Week of the Mournful Month of the year of the Klan LV.

Duly signed and sealed by His Majesty,

(Signed) WILLIAM JOSEPH SIMMONS,

Imperial Wizard.

Is this lunacy or charlatanism? Or both? It is so silly, and yet so serious. Chesterton has remarked, with his usual acumen, that those who take themselves most seriously are the insane. Perhaps, then, the Imperial Wizard should be committed to a madhouse rather than a jail. The Kleagles, and Klexters, and other nabobs should go with him. The rank and fire—the Klanfools—might then be sent to sanitariums to undergo treatment for gullibility.

But let us made no mistake. William Joseph Simmons may be as "mad as a March hare," but he is as shrewd as P. T. Barnum. He knows his America as well as Get-Rich-Quick Wallingford. We shall see this presently. But, meanwhile, let us have a bit of Klan melodrama.

"After fourteen years of preparation" (it is the original Imperial Wizard who is speaking), "on Thanksgiving Night in the year 1915, thirty-four intrepid spirits made their way to a mountain near Atlanta, and there on the mountain top, at the midnight hour, while men braved the surging blasts of the wild wintry mountain winds, and endured a temperature far below freezing, bathed in the sacred glow of the fiery cross, the Invisible Empire was called forth from its slumber of half a century."

O sacred recollections of the good old guileless days of melodrama! "It's a hard night on the banks, boys! Heaven help those who go down to the sea in ships on such a night as this!" "It's a hard night on the mountain top, boys! Heaven help the 'intrepid spirits' who brave the wintry blasts of a Thanksgiving Night in Georgia!"

Picture those patriots of the peak leaving the open fireplace, or the barber-shop stove, or the Union Station radiator, pressing on fearlessly by trolley to Stone

Mountain, twelve miles away, and climbing in a "temperature far below freezing" even to the very tip, reaching the dizzy altitude of eighteen hundred feet. How insignificant, by camparison, are the exploits of Peary, or Amundsen, or Robert Scott!

Unfortunately, at this point in the record, the Imperial Wizard's English becomes a bit blurred. We cannot tell whether it was the Invisible Empire, or the intrepid thirty-four, or the mountain top, that was "bathed in the sacred glow of the fiery cross." But though the syntax be somewhat scrambled, the story is, none the less, graphic and thrilling. Under the spell of the Wizard's words, the Invisible Empire becomes visible. We can see it, awaking like Rip Van Winkle, from its long sleep, stretching its arms, blinking in the light of the fiery cross, stiffly and laboriously rising to its feet, yawning wearily: "Ho! ho! there's bloody work to be done, negroes to be burned, solitary men to be tarred and feathered, women to be stripped and whipped. Yea, there's work for 'intrepid spirits' to do! Fe, fi, fo, fum!"

Or course, this sophisticated generation, which only laughs at melodrama, will ask irreverently: "Had the intrepid spirits no homes? Are there no halls to be hired in Atlanta? Would not the landlady let them use the back parlor for the evening? Or could they not have assembled on a vacant lot, safe and warm behind the billboards? Why should they go to the top of a mountain, far, far away in the suburbs?"

The Imperial Wizard has not recorded the message delivered that terrible night on the mountain top, but very probably it was in substance the same that he has frequently delivered ever since: "This great nation, with all it provides, can be snatched away from you between the rising and the setting of one sun . . . in

the space of one day, and that day of no more than
ten hours; when the hordes of aliens *walk to the ballot box (!)* and their votes outnumber yours, then
that alien horde has got you by the throat. Americans will awaken from their slumber and rush out
for battle. The soil of America will run red with the
blood of its people."[2]

I confess that I cannot visualize that scene as vividly
as the scene on the mountain top. The description is
rather puzzling. The "aliens" walk to the ballot box.
But if they are aliens and walk to the ballot box, they
will simply have to walk right home again. Aliens do
not vote in the United States. If the "aliens" vote,
they have been naturalized, and if they have been
naturalized, they are no longer "aliens," but citizens.
Are we to understand that the Klan is opposed to all
naturalization? And are they, then, opposed to the
Constitution, which legalizes naturalization?

It seems also that while the "aliens" are voting, the
"100 per cent Americans" are slumbering. Do the
"aliens" outnumber the Americans at the polls because the Americans take advantage of the holiday to
remain in bed? And are they who remain in bed on
Election Day one hundred per cent. Americans? Is it
blameworthy for naturalized citizens to exercise their
constitutional right to vote? It is all rather confus-
ing. However, the aliens seize the sleeping patriots by
the throat; the patriots awake; the soil of America
runs red with their blood. So much, at least, is clear.

I have, perhaps, insinuated that Simmons is insane.
But "though this be madness, yet there is method in
it." He is "but mad north-north-west: when the wind
is southerly," he knows "a hawk from a handsaw."
He knows which side of his bread is buttered. And

[2] *The Searchlight,* William Joseph Simmons. April 30, 1921.

he knows how to get the bread and butter. While he was still occupying the position of "Imperial Wizard," he claimed that there were two million members of the Klan. The initiation fee is, or was, $10.00 per head. For regalia, the Klanfools pay $6.50. But the regalia consists only of a nightgown and a mask, and is worth, perhaps, $1.50. Therefore, two million initiations produce a profit of thirty million dollars— and all this in five or six years. I have compared Simmons with Barnum and with Get-Rich-Quick Wallingford. But, after all, compared with the Imperial Wizard, Barnum and Wallingford were only tyros. Even the editors and owners of the *Menace* were, likewise, amateurs at money-making. Earl McClure made $100,000; W. L. Phelps made $300,000; Marvin Brown made $50,000. But what are the paltry sums of $100,000 or even $300,000, in fifteen or twenty years over against $30,000,000 in five years?

But let us not fail to notice that there is always a mine of religious bigotry, here in America, and that those who work it are sure of quick and substantial profits. Wallingford made his money on carpet tacks. Others go in for patent medicines. Still others invent a "sure cure for baldness." Recently, bootlegging has become the favorite path to sudden wealth. But of all frauds and "fakers," the "brewers of bigotry" are the shrewdest. They make money faster and more abundantly than any other kind of charlatans; and while they grow rich, they have the added consolation of being reputed patriots or saints, or both. Barnum was right. "The public loves to be humbugged." And Ben Franklin was right. "A fool and his money are soon parted." But the Imperial Wizards are not the fools. Nor the Grand Goblins, nor the Titans, nor the Kleagles, nor the Exalted Cyclops.

They are "getting theirs while the getting is good." The fools are those who pay $10.00 for initiation and $6.50 for a sheet.

However, it is time to be serious—though not too serious. There is always a tendency to maintain that any contemporary evil is "the worst ever." But there have been far worse outbursts of bigotry than that of the modern Ku-Klux Klan. It may be that the Klan has not yet reached the peak of its pernicious activities. Conditions may get worse before they get better. But it is a fact that thus far the Ku-Klux Klan has not accomplished nearly so much villainy as the "Native American" Movement, of the thirties and forties, or the "Know-nothing" Movement, of the fifties, in the last century. In those troublous times, when Catholics were as few all over the United States as they are now in the Southern States, they suffered more persecution than the Klan can possibly inflict today. Mobs were formed and ran riot everywhere, burning or dynamiting churches, convents, academies, and even hospitals.

In Philadelphia, in 1844, two Catholic churches were burned to the ground. Catholic worship was suspended, the homes of Catholics were invaded and destroyed and their occupants deliberately murdered.

At Cincinnati, a mob of six hundred, with firebrands and ropes, attacked the Cathedral, with intent to burn it and to hang a papal nuncio, who was the guest of the bishop. Similar disturbances, and worse, took place in dozens of other cities and towns. From Louisville, Bishop Spalding wrote in August 1855: "We have just passed through a reign of terror, surpassed only by the Philadelphia riots. Nearly one hundred poor Irish have been butchered or burned and some twenty houses have been consumed in the flames. The city authorities, all Know-nothings, looked calmly on, and they are now endeavoring to lay the blame on the Catholics."

Politically, too, the Know-nothings were active. In Philadelphia, Baltimore, New York, New Orleans, and San Francisco (to say nothing of scores of smaller cities), mayors were elected on anti-Catholic platforms. Fifteen States elected Know-nothing governors. In the Thirty-fifth Congress, which sat from 1857 to 1859, one hundred and thirteen representatives out of two hundred and thirty-six, were either actual members of the Know-nothing Party or Republicans who had been elected to office after an open declaration of their anti-Catholic convictions.

In the national election of 1852, the Know-nothings claimed to control 1,500,000 votes—half of the grand total.

But the Know-nothing Party collapsed as suddenly and as mysteriously as it had originated. When, in 1856, it nominated Millard Fillmore for the Presidency, he was ignominiously defeated, receiving only eight electoral votes, all of which were cast by one State, Maryland. There is consolation in that fact for those who are now worried about what may be the future for Catholics if the Klan continues to grow. Organized Bigotry, above all things else, is spasmodic. It comes in waves, but the waves finally—and suddenly—break. The Ku-Klux Klan, up to the present has had no such political success as the Know-nothings. It has voted the parochial school out of existence in Oregon, and elected a Senator from Texas, but, beyond that, it has achieved no very important results by the ballot.

As for crimes of violence attributable to members of the Klan, the New York *World*, which conducted a thorough and painstaking investigation, reports that in one year, October 1920, to September 1921, there were 4 murders, 1 "irreparable mutilation," 1 branding with acid, 41 floggings, 27 cases of tarring and feathering, and 5 kidnappings, by cloaked and hooded law-breakers in the United States.

In the year 1922, conditions were worse. Senator D. I. Walsh, of Massachusetts, addressing Attorney General Daugherty, quotes from a letter written to him by a lawyer in Texas:

"I do not think it would be an exaggeration to say that Texas has had, within the last eighteen months, five hundred tar and feather parties and whipping bees, not to mention a number of homicides, assaults, and other offenses directed against the person; threatening letters by the score have been given to the victims of this huge criminal conspiracy, ordering them, in many instances, to leave their homes; women have been tarred and feathered and old men in their dotage have not been spared their vengeance; young girls in their teens and not hardly in womanhood have been the victims of these letters, and, in many instances, they have been forced to leave their homes on account of the slander and ignominy heaped on them.

"So far as I know, not one of these criminals has been brought to justice. At Waco, the home of the Governor of Texas, police officers arrested three masked and hooded men with their victim, covered with hot tar and feathers, in their possession. The Grand Jury of McClennan County voted 'No bill.' In Dallas, a Klan stronghold, it is reported that at least fifty men have been whipped at one place. One man, prominent in the business life of the city, was taken from his home and away from his little motherless girls, and beaten. One of his children, a girl, was knocked down and injured while trying to defend her father.

"At Teneha, a woman was tarred and feathered and beaten with a wet rope, because she had married a second time. At Austin, the capital city of the State, numbers of outrages have been perpetrated upon individuals. Every little town, hamlet and city in the State, with but few exceptions, have had their little 'patriotic fêtes,' featuring hot tar, feathers, and wet ropes. It would astound the people of the United States if the truth about this organization in Texas could be given."

The Governor of Louisiana thought it necessary to make a personal visit to President Harding to ask federal coöperation in a campaign against the outrages of the Klan. While the Governor was at the Capital, alarming accounts were printed in the newspapers, declaring that "the invisible Empire" had grown to such an extent, and had so far usurped all power that the administration of law and order had become *"negligible"* in certain parts of the State of Louisiana. Governor Parker denounced these reports as exaggerations. But the actual seriousness of the situation, which led him to make his visit and his appeal to Washington, he did not deny.

The conditions existing in Texas and Louisiana fairly illustrate the state of the case throughout the South and Southwest. In the North, the Middle West, and parts of the far West, the Klansmen are equally virulent, and perhaps would be equally violent were it not that in these sections Catholics are too numerous to be seriously molested. Right there is a hint as to the principal characteristic of the Klansmen—their cowardice.

It is conceivable that a mob may sometimes be a

random aggregation of heroes. But a masked mob is always an aggregation of cowards. The French revolutionists, who stormed the Bastille, in the days of Louis XVI., were risking their lives. They were a mob only because they could not be an army. They wore no masks. The mob that came by night with swords and staves into the Garden of Gethsemane to apprehend Jesus Christ, wore no masks. Even Judas did not conceal his countenance. But a mob of men, who cover their faces with hoods and their forms with sheets, is a mob of cowards. When a man is afraid to show his colors, it must be because he is "yellow."

Furthermore, the Klan, in its attacks, never allows a man to have a fighting chance. One man never fights one man; the man must fight the mob. A mob that attacks an army, like the mob that precipitated the revolution in Russia, is certainly courageous. It is no lark to go armed only with pikes or pitchforks into the face of machine guns. The Bolsheviki may be savage, but they are not cowards. But the mobs of Klansmen that attack one solitary defenseless person are obviously cowards. If one gang of street boys attacks another gang, there may be "fair play" between them. But if a whole gang attacks one defenseless boy, the gang is despicable. If there were even an iota of chivalry in the heart of a Klansman, he would recognize that obvious fact.

They have no courage. Likewise they have no logic. They claim to be "100 per cent. American." The truth is that they would ruin America. There could not possibly be a more dangerous anti-American society than one which is a law unto itself. Obedience to law, observance of the established means of obtaining justice, acceptance of the decisions of the courts, are a *sine qua non* of the existence of our form of government. But the Ku-Klux Klan makes itself a police force, judge, jury, attorney, executioner, mayor, governor, supreme dictator in all matters pertaining not only to government, but to manners, morals, and religion. This arrogant society has taken the duty upon itself to warn gamblers, adulterers, "joy-riders;" to teach editors what they may write or publish; to dictate to judges on the bench about their decisions. It has violated the habeas corpus act. With the alleged purpose of punishing crime, it has been guilty of more serious crimes— unlawful seizure, abduction, punishment without trial. It is a state within the state, or rather a state above the state. Indeed, it claims to be that most dangerous of all institutions, an Invisible Empire. Being invisible, it is likewise intangible and irresponsible. If Louis XIV. ever said, *"L'Etat c'est moi,"* he spoke like a tyrant. The Ku-Klux Klan repeats the words attributed to the King, "I am the state."

The only possible justification of such a society would be the utter absence of law and order, a condition of anarchy with which the State is unable to cope. The Vigilance Committees of early days in Calfornia were necessitated and justified by the chaotic social conditions incidental to the rush for gold. No such conditions prevail now in any American State. So long as there is no condition of anarchy, there is no call for a Vigilance Committee, and still less is there any justification for a "Klan." The Klan will cause anarchy, not cure it.

Again, the K. K. K. is a menace to the peace of the country, because its wicked and violent methods might easily lead to retaliation. If the Klan antagonizes and persecutes Catholics, Jews and negroes, then Catholics and Jews and negroes have at least equal

13

right to antagonize their antagonists, and to persecute their persecutors. This will not be done—at least Catholics will not succumb to the temptation to correct crime with crime—but if the day does come when the Ku-Klux Klan becomes strong enough to nullify the administration of justice in any State, or in the Union, the Catholics, Jews and negroes will have to defend themselves in the most effective way possible. When the Know-nothings, in 1854, threatened to burn St. Patrick's Cathedral in New York, Bishop Hughes asked his legal advisers the question: "Does the State guarantee compensation for damages done by rioters?" The lawyers replied that the State makes no such guarantee. "Then," said the Bishop, "the State intends that the citizens shall defend their own property." And he published a declaration, saying that, "in case all other protection fail," Catholics should "defend their property even with their lives. In this, they will not be acting against, but for, the law."

That principle of self-defense is, of course, indefeasible. It may be brought into effect once again if the Ku-Klux Klan gets out of hand.

Catholics will not be driven to retaliation. But they may be driven to self-defense, even to the extent of bloodshed. It is natural, therefore, that governors and magistrates generally should bestir themselves to anticipate and to prevent the anarchical conditions that will prevail if the Klan is not soon interrupted in its dangerous and un-American campaign of disseminating racial and religious animosity.

MR. CARL SCHURZ AND HIS VICTIMS.

The KKK

Wants You!

www.ingramcontent.com/pod-product-compliance
Lightning Source LLC
Chambersburg PA
CBHW072030280526
45788CB00007B/2741